THE ROAD

A Book of inspirational Spiritual Poetry by Stephen W. Milhouse. His unique style of storytelling through use of rhyme, flow and verse will allow you (The Reader) to feel each stanza. This is Stephen's first complete book. Journey down "**The Road**" and find your "**Stranger**"... find yourself.

The Road

A compilation of 30 Poems

©2022 Stephen W Milhouse

Self-Published by Stephen Warren Milhouse

Chicago, IL

www.APoetryMan.com

StephenMilhouse@APoetryMan.com

The Author:

Stephen Warren Milhouse

Born July 6th 1959, to parents of unknown name, age, ethnicity, education, or origin.

Adopted and raised by an African American Christian/Catholic couple.

Stephen grew up on the "Westside" of Chicago during the 1960's. One of the roughest periods in Chicago's history, The Martin Luther King and John F. Kennedy assassination years.

Attended Public and Catholic Grammar and High School. Educated in "The Streets", and in "The Books".

Spending a brief time in the US AIR Force and Honorably Discharged, Stephen has spent equal time on opposing sides of society; both as business entrepreneur and homeless veteran; factory worker and Computer Technician. He brings this diverse, unique aspect to his writing. He writes from his heart so you feel...

"Every joy and every pain
  Each setback and every gain
  The Sunshine and The Rain.
  To live ...
  To love...
  To feel both stress and strain
  To watch your life go down ..."The Drain"
  To die...
  Then live to love life once again..."   (The Author)

Journey down "**The Road**" ...find out which "**Stranger**" you're walking with.

Stephen W. Milhouse

The Author

Table of Contents

THE ROAD

©by :Stephen Milhouse 01/10/87 Revised 09/30/96 & 02/28/10

AS I WAS WALKING DOWN
"THE ROAD"
A STRANGER CAME MY WAY
he ASKED WHERE I WAS GOING
I REALLY COULD NOT SAY

he SAID THAT he WOULD HELP
ME
IN ANY WAY he COULD
IF I WOULD ONLY WALK WITH
him
THOUGH I DID NOT FEEL I
SHOULD

I FOLLOWED him FOR QUITE
SOME TIME
he LED ME OFF *THE ROAD*
DOWN A WIDE WELL TRAVELED
PATHWAY
TO A VERY STRANGE ABODE . . .

A HOUSE UNEARTHLY EERIE
IN A PLACE AS DARK AS NIGHT
SENT SHIVERS UP AND DOWN MY
SPINE
AS I BEHELD THE SIGHT

he SAID his DOOR WAS *ALWAYS*
OPEN
AND BECKONED ME TO COME
I SAID THAT'S ALRIGHT MISTER
I'M NOT REALLY QUITE THAT
DUMB

he ASKED:
WHAT WOULD MAKE YOU SAY
THAT
I DON'T QUITE UNDERSTAND . . .
HAVE I NOT BEEN GOOD TO YOU
BY LENDING YOU A HAND?

I SAID:
IT'S TRUE YOU'VE BEEN MOST
KIND
BUT I DON'T KNOW YOUR NAME
I WOULD JUST AS SOON NOT GO
INSIDE
BUT RETURN THE WAY I CAME

he SAID:
my NAME IS NOT IMPORTANT
YOU MAY CALL me FRIEND
my DOOR IS *ALWAYS* OPEN
AND ALL ARE WELCOME TO COME
IN

I SAID:
APPRECIATE your OFFER SIR
BUT I'LL HAVE TO PASS TONIGHT
THERE ARE THINGS ABOUT
you and your house
THAT DO NOT SEEM QUITE
RIGHT

WHY WOULD A PERSON BUILD
A HOUSE IN A VALLEY DARK AS
NIGHT?
A HOUSE THAT HAS NO WINDOWS
IN A PLACE THAT HAS NO
LIGHT?

AND THOSE EERIE LOOKING
STATUES
you HAVE OUTSIDE your DOOR
BEASTLY LOOKING demons
THAT I'VE NEVER SEEN BEFORE!!

SO MANY THINGS ABOUT THIS
PLACE
JUST DO NOT MAKE MUCH SENSE
YOU DO NOT HAVE A NEIGHBOR
WHY HAVE A TWELVE FOOT
FENCE??

AND WHILE I'M ON THE SUBJECT...
ONE MORE THING I MUST CONFESS
I CAN NOT UNDERSTAND NOR READ
your *VERY STRANGE* ADDRESS.....

.......666 M A I L i V E D E H T

TOO MANY THINGS ABOUT you
JUST DO NOT SEEM TO FIT
THE STATUE, FENCE & STRANGE
ADDRESS
WITH NUMBERS TRIPLE SIX!!!

WITH THAT I LEFT THE stranger
AND RETURNED BACK UP THE HILL

ARRIVING AT THE TOP

I FOUND MY SELF LOST STILL

I MET ANOTHER STRANGER
NOT LIKE THE one BEFORE

AND INSTANTLY I FELT SOMEHOW
THAT I COULD TRUST HIM MORE

HE SPOKE IN PURE MAJESTIC
FASHION
AND HIS VOICE COULD NOT VOICE
LIES...

THE one YOU MET BEFORE ME
WAS the devil IN DISGUISE
he ASKED OF YOU THIS QUESTION
TO WHERE DO YOU NOW GO?
YOU PAUSED BUT ONE BRIEF
MOMENT
AND SAID YOU DID NOT KNOW
he LED YOU OFF TO his domain
A PLACE OF GRIEF AND STRIFE
IF YOU HAD GONE INSIDE his house
YOU WOULD HAVE LOST YOUR
LIFE

BUT I WAS WITH YOU BY YOUR
SIDE THIS CAN NOT BE IGNORED
FOR I AM JESUS CHRIST THY KING
THY SAVIOR AND THY LORD
IT TAKES BUT ONE BRIEF MOMENT
FOR YOU TO GET OFF TRACK
BUT LESS THAN ONE BRIEF
MOMENT
FOR FAITH IN ME TO BRING YOU
BACK

I SAID: FOR ALL THESE YEARS MY
LORD
I'VE SINNED REPEATEDLY
PLEASE TELL ME WHY YOU'VE
TAKEN
ALL THESE YEARS TO COME TO
ME??
THE LORD SAID:

FOR ALL THESE YEARS
AND MORE MY CHILD
WITH YOU I HAVE BEEN
AND IT HAS TAKEN
ALL THESE YEARS
FOR YOU...
TO LET ME IN

"THE ROAD MAP"

I WAS LOST AND SO CONFUSED

WHILE ON **THE ROAD** ONE DAY

I WAS *DRIVING IN MY CAR*

AND SOMEHOW LOST MY WAY

I KNEW I NEEDED SOMETHING

TO HELP ME FIND *DIRECTION*

PURPOSE ....

MOTIVATION ....

UNDERSTANDING ....

AND *PROTECTION*

THE *GLOVE COMPARTMENT* OPENED

AND THERE TO MY SURPRISE

WAS A ***BIBLE*** I'D FORGOTTEN

STARING ME RIGHT IN MY EYES

THE ROAD MAP THAT I NEEDED

TO HELP ME FIND MYSELF

THAT COULD NOT HELP ME

ONE SINGLE BIT

IF IT STAYED THERE ON THE SHELF

I OPENED UP **THE BIBLE**

AND I BEGAN TO READ IT

INSTANTLY I KNEW

IT WAS EXACTLY WHAT I NEEDED

GOD'S WORD THAT I WOULD

ALWAYS KEEP ....

AND READ

AT ANY COST

THE ROAD MAP I WOULD

ALWAYS USE TO KEEP FROM ....

"GETTING LOST".

"TIME"

TIME MOVES EVER FORWARD

AT A NEVER ENDING PACE

THERE IS NO SUCH THING AS...

TOO MUCH TIME

NOR ANY *TIME TO WASTE*

A SECOND....

MINUTE....

HOUR

A DAY....

A MONTH....

OR YEAR

DOESN'T MATTER VERY MUCH

IF YOU CAN NOT SPEND IT "HERE"

MANY MEN HAVE COME AND GONE

I WONDER HOW THEY FEEL

I WONDER IF THEY'RE NOW IN hELL

If *HEAVEN* IS FOR REAL

I'VE READ THE AVERAGE MAN ALIVE SPENDS

TWENTY YEARS ASLEEP

TWENTY YEARS HE GIVES AWAY

THE *REST* HE GETS TO KEEP

DON'T TAKE YOUR TIME FOR GRANTED

BECAUSE YOU NEVER KNOW

WHEN ITS TIME TO SAY GOODBYE

AND TIME FOR YOU TO GO

ANYTHING CAN HAPPEN

IT'S STRICTLY LEFT TO CHANCE

HERE TODAY THEN GONE AWAY

THRU UNSEEN CIRCUMSTANCE

WISELY USE THE TIME YOU HAVE

EACH AND EVERY DAY

BEFORE THE "SECOND HAND" OF TIME

SWEEPS YOUR TIME AWAY

Every Precious Moment

Every Precious Moment of everything we do

Contributes to the "Treasure Chest" I'm saving up for you

Overflowing Chest of Memories

Each special all alone

When added up together

They reflect The Love that's shown

Just like a well kept garden

That is tended tenderly

This is how our GOD intended

All of us to be

Cherish…

Every Precious Moment

Of Every Precious Day

And…

Every Precious Moment

You get the chance to say…

To Every Precious Loved One….

To Every Precious Love…..

"I Love You" …

And you're every bit as Precious

As Our Precious LORD Above   ©By: Stephen Milhouse 09/18/10

Our GOD is So Amazing

GOD is So Amazing

Worthy worshiping

And praising...

Each day My Love

For JESUS ever grows

Even as I'm dressing

Or on my knees professing

I never mind confessing...and

The LORD my GOD and SAVIOR surely knows

Just how much I Love HIM

Worship and Adore HIM

For increasingly and exceedingly it shows

Shows in all my action

The total satisfaction

That I know HIM and I say it

In this poem...rhyme and prose

With all the Love I can afford

I'll forever Praise The Lord

For truly is HE ever Worth The Praising

This for certain is The Truth

And I am all The Living Proof That...

JEHOVAH ...The LORD...

"OUR GOD IS SO AMAZING"

A LETTER TO GOD

WHEN MY FAITH IN **GOD** IS TESTED
THROUGH THE HARDSHIPS I ENDURE
WHEN I'M WEARY AND I'M LONELY
FEELING WEAK AND INSECURE
I LIFT MY HEAD TOWARD **HEAVEN**
AND ON MY KNEES I PRAY
TO **ALMIGHTY GOD THE FATHER**
AND THIS IS WHAT I SAY....

Dear **FATHER**,
LORD and **MASTER**

PLEASE HEAR ME AS I SPEAK
FATHER GIVE ME STRENGTH TO MAKE IT
TO THE GLORY THAT I SEEK
FATHER KEEP **YOUR HAND** UPON ME
EVERY SECOND
EVERY DAY
KEEP ME WALKING STRAIGHT TO YOU **LORD**
PLEASE DON'T LET ME STRAY
LORD WHEN I'M DOWN
LORD PICK ME UP
LORD WHEN I NEED A HAND
WHEN I DON'T SEE MY PURPOSE **LORD**
PLEASE MAKE ME UNDERSTAND
GIVE ME STRENGTH AND WISDOM **LORD**
TO LET **YOUR WILL BE DONE**
I LOVE YOU **FATHER JESUS**

SINCERELY SIGNED,
YOUR SON

©BY: STEPHEN MILHOUSE DECEMBER 28,1986

"Father Help me live my life"

Father help me live my life

Like I'm on camera every moment of the day

Help me find the words I'm seeking

When on my knees I pray

Convict my Spirit… Father

Should I pause to pick my nose

Help me search to find a "Kleenex"

When I could have used my clothes

Purge the wicked thoughts right out me

When people tick me off

When their mouths they do not cover

When they open it to cough

When I see a handsome stranger

As he walks so handsomely

Let not my lustfulness arise

To get the best of me

Father help me live my life

Like I'm on camera each moment of the night

When my nature is to do The Wrong

Convict me to do The Right

Rules For Married Christians
1st Peter Chapter 3

Wives obey your husbands

husbands love your wives

and you will be rewarded

with rich fulfilling lives

respect each other always

procreate with love

and you'll receive your blessings

from The Father up above

love each other dearly

with a mind that has no pride

love with the kind of love

that can't be held inside

do all these things together

and together be as one

and the Lord will bless you further

with a daughter or a son

when you have your children

teach them every single day

give them love and understanding

teach them how to pray

give them GOD...

and GOD will give you

peace and love forevermore

love that's not forgotten

when you "Knock on Heavens Door

©by: Stephen Milhouse

March 04, 1987

HE SET ME UPON A ROCK

Psalm 27 verses 5 -14

Set me upon a rock

and I will fear no beast nor man

Set me upon a rock

and there is where I'll stand

For in the time of trouble

THE GOOD SHEPARD tends HIS flock

and I will fear no evil

HE set me upon a rock

Set me upon a rock

and I'll stand forever more

though a Hurricane be blowin'

tidal waves against my door

I will stand there firm....

unyielding

I will stand there on the shore

with all my earthly treasures

tied securely to the dock

I will fear no evil

HE set me upon a rock

Set me upon a rock

and there is where I'll stay

Set me upon a rock

forever and a day

as the "*second hand*" of Time

ticks the minutes off the clock

I will fear no evil

HE Set Me Upon A Rock

©By: Stephen Milhouse

February 06, 1986

Revised: February 28, 2010

LIKE SHEEP WITHOUT A SHEPHERD

We're *Like Sheep without a Shepard*

roaming wild throughout the land

useless to each other....

like an "arm" without a "hand"

like a "plan" without a "purpose"

like a "dream" without a "goal"

like a "room" without a "candle"

like a "man" without a "soul"

like a "word" without a "meaning"

like a "nail" without a "board"

like a "book" without an "ending"

like we are without The LORD

without JESUS....

we are hopeless....

heartless....

hapless....

helpless men

in a world filled with temptation

in a world that's filled with sin

CHRIST is all that stands between us

and eternal pain and strife

HE can give you true salvation

and eternal peace and life

accept CHRIST as your SAVIOR

don't wait another *minute*

for one *second* spent in Heaven

beats *fifty-nine* you'd spend not in it

Thirsty For You LORD

LORD...
My Soul is Thirsty
I'm... **Thirsty for YOU LORD**
The Enemy surrounds me
My prayers have been ignored
FATHER quench The Fire in me
FATHER save me from their sword
Spiritually fulfill me
I'm ...**Thirsty For YOU LORD**

I need YOU FATHER JESUS...
So on my knees I pray
That my cup would runneth over
Each and every day
Let not the sun set nightly
Without a Word from YOU
I need YOUR LIVING WATERS
To do what I should do
The desert of my Soul
Is parched and unexplored
I need YOU FATHER JESUS
I'm... **Thirsty FOR YOU LORD**

The Spirit of Truth

The Spirit of Truth is a SPRIRIT

And you will know The TRUTH

When you hear it

The Spirit is of GOD

Not from the devil

Above all reproof

And on the level

It has illumination of its own

 A Light that burns so bright

It must be shown

By GOD's Command

The TRUTH must Stand

 And Stand alone

It can't be hidden or divided

And even when decided

By a judge I still have proof

That the words that I have written

 Whether you say I did or didn't

The fact remains

And will not change…

The fact:

They are The Truth

©By: Stephen Milhouse -07-27-09

Jesus Guides My Hand

The Lord is in my every thought

Lord Jesus guides my hand

He helps me write these words you read

He helps you understand

Keep Thy Hand upon me Lord

Keep me free from sin

Let me write Your Word Divine

Lord Jesus guide my pen

I hear You when I'm wide awake

and when I'm fast asleep

I can't control the words I hear

Into my mind they leap

You must be writing through me Lord

For no matter who's around

Words of wisdom come to me

I have to write them down

As fast as I can write one Word

another comes to mind

It just has to be You Jesus

Teaching me Your Word Divine

I do not know your purpose Lord

I know not Your intent

I only know The Words I write

Are straight from Heaven sent

Until I know the answer

I'll question You no more

I'll just continue writing

As I've never wrote before

By Stephen Milhouse

January 18, 1987

"FOOD FOR THOUGHT"

HAVE YOU EVER WONDERED

WHO PUT US HERE ON EARTH

HOW WE WERE CREATED THRU

THE MIRACLE OF BIRTH

HOW CAN WE ASK THESE QUESTIONS

WHAT CAUSES US TO THINK

WHO GAVE US SEEDS OF KNOWLEDGE

HOW COME WE HAVE TOO BLINK

HAVE YOU EVER NOTICED

ALL THINGS IN PERFECT TUNE

ALL THINGS UNIQUELY BALANCED

THE SUN

THE EARTH

AND MOON

HOW EVERYTHING WE NEED TO LIVE

IS FURNISHED NITE AND DAY

AIR WE BREATH ...

WATER WE DRINK ...

THE LIGHT WHICH GUIDES OUR WAY

EVERYTHING WE NEED TO LIVE

IS RIGHT HERE ON THE PLANET

SO MUCH SOMETIMES

WE MAY FORGET

AND TAKE THESE THINGS FOR GRANTED

WOULD YOU AGREE

THIS MYSTERY

IS NO FREAK ACCIDENT

BUT ALL A PART OF GODS OWN PLAN

AND STRAIGHT FROM HEAVEN SENT

When I look in the Mirror

When I look in the Mirror

Who do I see?

A reflection of me

Or reflection of WE?

If the I that I see

Is not the WE it should be

Then unlock the chains

And set yourself free

Somewhere down The Road

I found myself lost

Forgot about Christ

Who died on The Cross

And paid for my sin

So I could look in the mirror

And see WE again

"The Lord Is My Comfort"
"The Lord Is My Shepard"

The Lord is my Comfort

My "pillow" at night

HE takes on my battles

and wins all my fights

All that I cherish

HE holds in HIS Arms

Protecting and keeping them

Safe from all harm

The Lord is my Shepard

When I'm led astray

He "finds" me

And leads me back

To the right way

All of my sorrow

and all of my pain

The Lord makes become ...

Joyous Spiritual gain ©By: Stephen Milhouse December 11, 1987

Mother's Love is Mine

Mama taught me …

How to write my ABC's

And …

Kissed me on my "skinned up" knees

Made me less afraid of bees

Taught me to say "thanks" and "please"

That's why with every passing thought

I think about the things you taught

The little things that make me cry

And how sad I'll feel the day you die

But knowing that you know this now

"Unsaddens" some of the sad somehow

And turns it into something proud

To know I'll see your face in every cloud

And know you'll be looking down on me

With a Mother's Love the World can see

And As I write these words that rhyme

I'm so glad your…Mother's Love is Mine

The Hole in my Heart

The Hole in my Heart
Kept increasing
Like the pain that I felt without ceasing
Not a moment goes by
Nor the tears that I cry
We own nothing in life
We're just leasing

Our life here on The Earth is but fleeting
Here then gone
In a Beat of the Heart in our chest
That's now beating
Each beat was numbered by GOD before time
Before I ever considered this rhyme
Before our souls ever crossed
Before our terrible lost
Before we met at our predestined meeting

Now you're gone after all of these years
My eyes have cried the last tear of my tears
I feared time would never stop them from tearing
I might fear we're forever apart...
The end predetermined... even be`fore the start
The indescribable hurt
The Earth and all of its dirt
Could never refill The Hole that you've left in My Heart
But my Faith in my GOD puts to rest all the fears I was fearing

The Very Thought of You

I LOVE YOU DAD

In a way that words cannot express

The way you walk

The way you talk

The way you smile

The way you dress

Your unique style

You are The Best

Husband, Neighbor, Father... Grandpa, Partner, Friend

The Best Dad a son could ever hope for

Someone on whom you can depend

No one could ask for more

My eyes begin to water

As I watch you pass another year

I'm deeply saddened and dare I say... I shed a little tear

For I know one day... The Day will come

Day most I greatly fear

When I will need a hug from you

And Dad you won't be here

But where you are in Heaven

Just know that this is true

I will cherish every moment that we've had together

Every laugh and every cry

And ...**The Very Thought of You**

Dad...Will never die

By: Stephen Milhouse 03-27-2012   You're forever in my Heart

REMEMBER

REMEMBER ALL THE GOOD TIMES

REMEMBER ALL THE BAD

REMEMBER ALL THE JOYOUS TIMES

REMEMBER ALL THE SAD

REMEMBER ALL THE UP TIMES

REMEMBER ALL THE DOWN

REMEMBER EVERY MOVE I MADE

REMEMBER EVERY SOUND

REMEMBER ALL THE TIMES WE LAUGHED

AND ALL THE TIMES WE CRIED

REMEMBER ALL THE TIMES

WE MADE EACH OTHER SATISFIED

REMEMBER ALL THE FUN WE HAD

TOGETHER YOU AND I

AND REMEMBER TOO

REMEMBER TO ....

NEVER EVER

SAY GOODBYE

REMEMBER THAT I TOLD YOU

NEVER TO FORGET

NOT A SINGLE SECOND SPENT TOGETHER

SHOULD YOU EVER HAVE REGRET

FOR IF YOU JUST REMEMBER

THEN I'VE NEVER TRULY DIED

AS LONG AS YOU REMEMBER TO

REMEMBER ME INSIDE

©BY STEPHEN MILHOUSE

DECEMBER 30 1986

"When all you ever really needed was a Hug"

YOU CANNOT BUY DISTRACTION

OR FAKE A CHILD'S REACTION

WITH A BIKE, A BAT, A BALL OR TOY

AND IT DOESN'T REALLY MATTER

IF THEY HAVE TO USE A LADDER

TO REACH YOUR ARMS TO SEE YOUR LOVING FACE

FOR IF THE TRUTH BE TOLD

Then you never get too old

To miss your mom or father's warm embrace

For whether girl or boy

This true fact you must deploy without a shrug

That no drink or words or drug

Could fill The Hole

That Can't Be Plugged

"When all you ever really needed was a Hug"

Relationship Bliss

You need GOD to know
Love...

And **Love** to have **Life**

If you wish to be happy and married

With a house and a spouse

Pray to **GOD** for a wife

Your attempts to find **Love** in a bar or online

Will leave you flat broke

Crazy out of your mind

There is only ***One*** place

And that place is **Prayer**

If you're looking for **Love**

You **will** find it there

This fact you must face

I can promise you this

You could search high and low and still you would miss

Searching and searching

Leaving no stone unturned

And after you've turned one hundred and four you could

continue to search for one hundred years more

Old Man or Old Maid

Heart Jaded and Burned

Now comes the lesson

I'm hoping You've learned

Bought and paid for in **Heaven**

Neither deserved or earned

The way to true **Love** is no **hit or miss**

It doesn't start out having sex...

Or begin with a kiss

...............BUT...............

If It **starts** with a **Prayer**

I can promise you this:
You'll be well on your way to

"Relationship Bliss" ©Stephen.Milhouse
09/10/2013

Life is a Spirit

Life is a Spirit
What does life matter?
JESUS CHRIST is THE CAKE
FATHER GOD is THE BATTER
Life is GOD
And GOD is LIFE....
Spirit Goodness
Never Strife
Love is Life
Life is Love
Love is GOD
GOD is LOVE
Real is GOD
GOD is REAL
GOD and JESUS CHRIST Can Heal
Provide to Man
Salvation Shield
All your needs fulfilled thru GOD
Satan's curse
One big façade
Trust in GOD
"In GOD We Trust"
"Say no to drugs"
Sin...sex...and lust
Unwed sex is death to Spirit
You may not agree
Not want to hear "IT"
Hear "IT" now ....
Hear "IT" well
Be alive....
And live to tell
AIDS is Real...
If you _fear_ "IT"
Live life on Earth...
And Not as a Spirit

By: Stephen Milhouse 08-02-09 revised 03-17-10

REVELATION

I tell you CHRIST is
coming
CHRIST will come again
to pass HIS *FINAL
JUDGEMENT*
and cleanse the world of sin
Seventeen signs warn us
that CHRIST is on HIS way
we can not know the hour
the second
or the day

The 1st sign will be *people*
people every day
*using CHRIST's MOST
HOLY NAME*
in a false deceitful way

The 2nd sign is *war*
and a lot of *talk of war*
more nations fighting
nations
than there has ever been
before

The 3rd is *people starving*
people starving every day
nations that could feed the
world
with the food they throw
away

The 4th sign will be
Earthquakes
occurring everywhere
devastating mass
destruction
cities burned beyond repair

The 5th sign will be
Christians
killed because of their belief
in JESUS CHRIST THE
SON OF GOD
who makes all suffering
brief

The 6th sign will be *people*
giving up to turn away
forgetting how to love
forgetting how to pray

The 7th sign is happening
now
even as I speak ....
false religious teachers
fooling people every week

The 8th sign will be *people*
breaking laws and sinning
bold
with no forethought or
emotion
because their hearts are cold

The 9th sign ....
sinners saying everything is
safe and fine
when all the while they grin
and smile
sin's working overtime

The 10th sign will be *people*
loving money and
themselves
hiding money in their
mattress
or in books they keep on
shelves
hiding money in their shoes
and socks
hiding money in the wall
any place that they might
dream or find
in any place at all

Sign 11 will be *children*
and young adults alike
disrespectful to their
parents
telling them to take a hike

12 is *people so unholy*
so ungrateful it's a shame
thankless GODLESS
people
whose whole lives are lived
in pain

13 is the next sign
that should be thought
about

next time you have a party
or decide to party out
people world-wide over
will love fun instead of
GOD
people hating one another
their whole lives one big
facade

14 is the next sign
of JESUS CHRIST'S return
good news of GOD THE
FATHER
made so everyone can learn
every single nation
must know about THE
LORD
no nation will be left untold
no one must be ignored

Jews returning to their
homeland
will be the 15th sign
every single Jew on earth
and adopted Jew you find
in any country anywhere
in any place or time
will disappear from anyone
not knowing GOD
and leave them far behind

Think about the 16th sign
next time you visit Vegas
for *the desert will be full of*
joy
and become like an oasis

The last and final sign
of what GOD has in store
Is people going places
that they've never gone
before

There is something else in
Daniel
Chapter 12 verse number 4
people will know more
things
than they've ever known
before ©By: Stephen Milhouse - March 08,
1987

THE LORD HE IS YOUR LIGHT

THE LORD will light the way for you

in the darkest night

with evil on the left of you

HE keeps you on the right

THE MIGHTY NAME OF JESUS

will make your pathway straight

HIS AWESOME ENDLESS LOVE

will always conquer hate

should enemies surround you

to do you evil harm

THE LORD will keep you cradled

in HIS strong yet gentle arms

you walk right through the "circle"

without a single scratch

THE LORD protects you

with the strength

no foe could hope to match

your foes are vanquished

one by one

felled by unseen fist

THE LORD defeats them with HIS LOVE

no foe could conquer this

call on JESUS' MIGHTY NAME

anytime you have to fight

THE NAME .... ABOVE ALL OTHER NAMES

THE LORD HE IS YOUR LIGHT

©BY: Stephen Milhouse

December 14, 1986 Revised November 10, 2002 re-revised January 18, 2008

I MET THE HOLY GHOST

I once was a *backslider*
who slid from coast-to-coast
until one day while *on The Road*
I MET THE HOLY GHOST

I met HIM at a *"truck stop"* (dope house)
where I'd stopped to grab some *chow*
in a blinding flash HE came
so fast I knew not how

I found an empty parking place
and quickly parked my car
that's when I heard a *voice* ask me
"DO YOU KNOW WHERE YOU ARE?"

I did not pay attention
"just the radio", I said
and headed for *the diner*
with but one thought in my head

The *waitress* took my *order*
and I found myself a seat
all at once HE hit me
and knocked me off my feet

I looked in all directions
to see who'd knocked me down
but much to my surprise
a single soul could not be found

I said, "What the heck is
happening??!!"
"What the hell is going on??"
"Whoever's playing games with me
won't be playing very long!!"

I shouted at the *waitress*
to hurry with my *chow!*
"keeeep your shirt on sir", she said
"I'm fixing it right now!"

I mumbled something to myself
and sat back in my seat
that's when I heard *THE VOICE* again
that knocked me off my feet!!

THE VOICE resounded loudly
so loud IT hurt my ear...
*"LEAVE THOU FROM HERE
QUICKLY"*
*"THOU DOST BELONG NOT
HERE!!!!"*

I tried to disbelieve it
A figment of my mind
that would leave and go away
if only given time

just then ....
THE VOICE repeated
this time *MAJESTICALLY*
then all at once I knew ...

THE HOLY GHOST had come to me

my face profusely sweated
I stood there petrified
THE VOICE said ...

"BE THOU NOT AFRAID MY CHILD
AND BE NOT TERRIFIED
OPEN UP THY HEART TO ME
AND LET ME LIVE INSIDE
AND I WILL KEEP THEE SAFE
FROM SIN
AND ALWAYS BE THY GUIDE
THY FATHER LOVED THEE
FROM THY BIRTH
AND KNEW THOU NEEDETH MOST
TO REPENT THEE ALL THY SIN
AND RECEIVE THE HOLY GHOST"

I got back in my car
and drove from coast-to-coast

this time ...
not as a sinner
because ....

I MET THE HOLY GHOST

BY: STEPHEN MILHOUSE
       JANUARY 10, 1987

GOD Gives You What You Need

The LORD is always conscious
and mindful of our needs
Watching over each of us
as the farmer does his seeds

Everything we need to live
and love and worship CHRIST
is furnished without end
We needn't ever ask HIM twice

Still many call on GOD
to aid a lustful deed
The Lord denies this sinful wish
no matter how we plead

It's not that HE can't hear you
He hears your every thought
It's just that He won't answer
You're not living as HE taught

Many of you thought of GOD while smokin' "crack" or "weed"
"Shooting" heroin or "coke" or doing "*hits of speed*"
If you're still here ….
alive on earth after you've ODed
I know that you will testify
GOD gives you what you need

The TEN Commandments
wrote for us
with GOD'S Almighty Hand
teach us how we each should live
and treat our fellow man

GODS Word and law wrote down for man
you only need to read
and you will know without a doubt …

God Gives You What You Need

Self Published by Stephen W. Milhouse

A Logical Choice LLC

www.APoetryMan.org

stephenmilhouse@APoetryMan.org

The End